Your Book of Card Games

The YOUR BOOK Series

Acting
Aeromodelling
Animal Drawing
Aquaria
Astronomy
Badminton
Basketball
Bridges
Butterflies and Moths
Camping
The Way a Car Works
Card Games
Card Tricks
Chemistry
Chess
Coin Collecting
Computers
Confirmation
Contract Bridge
Mediaeval and Tudor Costume
17th & 18th Century Costume
19th Century Costume
Dinghy Sailing
Diving
The Earth
Electronics
Embroidery
Engines and Turbines
The English Bible
Fencing
Figure Drawing
Fishes
Flower Arranging
Flower Making
Flying
Freshwater Life
Furniture
Golf
Gymnastics
Heraldry
Hockey
Hovercraft
The Human Body
Judo
Kites
Knitted Toys
Knitting and Crochet
Knots
Landscape Drawing
Light
Magic
Maps and Map-Reading
Mental Magic
Model Car Racing
Modelling
Money
Music
Paper Folding
Parliament
Party Games
Patience
Pet Keeping
Photography
Photographing Wild Life
Keeping Ponies
Puppetry
The Recorder
Roman Britain
Rugger
The Seashore
Self-Defence
Sewing
Shell Collecting
Skating
Soccer
Sound
Space Travel
Squash
Stamps
Surnames
Survival Swimming and Life Saving
Swimming
Swimming Games and Activities
Table Tennis
Tape Recording
Television
Tennis
Trampolining
Trees
Underwater Swimming
Veteran and Edwardian Cars
Vintage Cars
Watching Wild Life
Waterways
Weather
Weaving
Woodwork

Your Book of

CARD GAMES

EWART KEMPSON

FABER AND FABER LIMITED
3 Queen Square London

First published in 1966
by Faber and Faber Limited
3 Queen Square London WC1
Reprinted 1973
Printed in Great Britain by
Latimer Trend & Company Ltd Plymouth

ISBN 0 571 06873 1

Contents

Introduction *page* 9
Preliminaries 11
Aces Low 13
Beggar My Neighbour 14
Donkey 16
Menagerie 18
Old Maid 20
Snap 21
Snip—Snap—Snorem 22
Eights 23
Go Fishing 26
I Doubt It 28
I Fancy My Cards 31
Nap 33
Pelmanism 36
The Earl of Coventry 38
Bridge—Two-handed 39
Fall Out 42
Newmarket 44
Oh! Well 46
Patience—Rescuing Cards 49
Poker Patience 51
Patience—The Shuffle 53

Plates

between pages 28 and 29

1. Preliminaries
2. Menagerie
3. Pelmanism
4. Oh! Well—End of Game
5. Patience—Rescuing Cards

6, 7. Poker Patience

Introduction

My parents considered that card games were good training for children, but I did not know I was being trained and disciplined until some years later or I might not have taken to Beggar My Neighbour, Snap and Old Maid quite as readily as I did. Suggest to some children that a card game is a lesson and they will shun cards for life. It is rather like the brave men and women who break ice in order to plunge into a lake. They do it 'for fun'; but if they were told they *had* to do it, some of them would look upon it as a most unpleasant imposition. Others would mutiny.

Without doubt card games are splendid training for the very young provided there is sufficient supervision to prevent the loser from shedding tears and the winner from gloating. In other words children should get into the way of losing with fortitude and of winning with grace. They should appreciate and cherish fair play.

It never occurred to me to ask who invented Beggar My Neighbour, Animal Noises, The Earl of Coventry and all the other games I played. My acknowledgements, therefore, go to unknown men and women who took the trouble to invent most of the games in this book, which are suitable for children of all ages, from 4 to 104.

The youngest children, say from five to eight years of age, will probably enjoy best:

Aces Low — Menagerie
Beggar My Neighbour — Old Maid
Donkey — Snap
Snip—Snap—Snorem

Children between the ages of nine and twelve may prefer:

Eights — I Fancy My Cards
Go Fishing — Nap
I Doubt It — Pelmanism
The Earl of Coventry

Those in the teens will almost certainly enjoy every game, but may have preference for:

Two-handed Bridge	Oh! Well
Fall Out	Newmarket
Rescuing Cards	Shuffle

Preliminaries

The first thing is to remember that playing-cards enjoy being handled by girls, boys and adults whose fingers are clean. Few things in a card game are worse than the discovery of a small portion of plum jam on the eight of spades, except, perhaps, a small portion of blackberry and apple jam, which I personally dislike even more than plum.

It is much easier to explain a game if everyone sits at the table and listens for a minute or two.

There are various ways of deciding who the dealer shall be. One way is to allow anyone to deal, for it doesn't really matter who gives out the cards. Another way is for anyone to deal cards face up to the players, and the first player to be dealt a jack is the first to deal. Yet another way is for anyone to deal one card, face up, to each player, and the player who receives the highest card deals first.

It seems best to adopt, and stick to, one method for all games, and it is just as easy to adopt a good method as it is to adopt a slipshod method. The cards should be shuffled and then spread face down across the table. When each player has drawn one card, all the drawn cards are exposed. The player with the highest card deals. The four cards at each end of the pack should not be drawn. (*See* Plate 1.)

In games where the deal passes from player to player, the rotation is always to the left, and the same applies to dealing. Unless otherwise stated, the first card of each deal goes to the player on the dealer's immediate left.

The cards are dealt one at a time, for there is no good reason why they should be dealt in twos or threes, although such variations are used.

When there are trumps in a game, it seems best to cut the cards to decide on the trump suit. The dealer or the player on the dealer's right takes off a portion of cards from a pack and shows the underneath card to the players. The suit of that card is the trump suit. A variation is for the dealer to turn up his own last card, that card deciding the trump suit. There is no advantage in this method, in fact there may be a distinct disadvantage at times.

Aces Low

This game for the *very* young is simply an introduction to numbers.

Each child is given four cards and one of them is told to lead his highest card. The others, in turn, play a card and the highest card in the suit led wins the trick. There are no trumps. The winner of a trick leads to the next trick.

The player who wins most tricks is, of course, the winner.

For the first dozen or so games, it is best to treat the aces as ones, the lowest cards in the pack: thus a two or any higher card beats a one. The kings, therefore, are the highest cards, and some instruction will be necessary regarding kings, queens and jacks.

Once they have the hang of the game they may be told to treat the aces as the highest cards; also trumps may be introduced.

Beggar My Neighbour

From two to six may play.

The player who draws the highest card from a spread pack deals the cards, face down, one at a time as far as they will go. It does not matter if some players hold a card more than other players.

Each player collects his cards and makes them into a packet which he places face down in front of him.

Tom, the player on the left of the dealer, goes first. He takes the top card from his packet of cards and places it face up on the centre of the table. Sally, the next player, places the top card from her packet face up on top of Tom's card. Mary, who is next, places her top card face up on Sally's card and so on until one of the players places an ace or a king or a queen or a jack face up. The next player has to pay

4 cards for an ace
3 cards for a king
2 cards for a queen
1 card for a jack

Let us take a look at a game:

	Tom	Sally	Mary	Tim
1st round	♠ 2	♡ 8	♠ 7	◇ 9
2nd round	♡ 4	♣ Q		

Mary, the next player, has to pay Sally two cards and she must play these cards on top of the queen, one at a time. If neither of Mary's pay-off cards is an ace, a king, a queen or a jack, Sally gathers up *all* the cards in the centre of the table (in the above case, eight) and places them at the bottom of her packet. But if either of the cards Mary pays in payment is an ace, a king, a queen or a jack, Sally loses this pay-off because Tim now has to pay Mary.

Suppose, therefore, that the first of Mary's two pay-off cards is an ace. Now Tim has to pay Mary four cards and if none of these four cards is A or K or Q or J, Mary takes all the cards in the centre of the table and places them at the bottom of her packet.

The excitement increases if Tim, while paying Mary, produces one of the four top cards. Now Tom has to pay Tim and whoever wins this pay-off will get a rich haul.

Although an ace receives four cards, a jack is a much more valuable card. The pay-off for a jack is only one card. Take the above case and assume that Tim, when paying off Mary, produces a king. Tom starts to pay off and produces an ace. Sally starts to pay off four cards to Tom and produces a jack. Mary has to pay only one card for a jack and it is much more likely to be a low card than one of the top cards. In fact it is a low card and Sally's haul includes five pay-off cards: her own queen of clubs and the jack she has just played, plus the pay-off cards that Mary, Tim and Tom played.

When a pay-off is completed, the payer plays the first card to the next round. As soon as a player has no more cards to play, he drops out of the game. In due course one player obtains all 52 cards and is the winner.

Donkey

Any number from three to thirteen may play. The best number of players is six.

The cards are sorted into fours of a kind: four aces, four kings, four queens and so on. If only three are playing, then only three lots of four (the aces, kings and queens) are required. If five are playing, the four jacks and the four tens are also required. If 13 are playing, the whole pack is required.

Any cards not required should be put back in their box and placed to one side.

You must try to be the first to collect four cards of the same rank and you must also be on the alert to avoid becoming the Donkey.

Anyone shuffles and deals the appropriate number of cards one at a time, face down, starting with the player on his left.

Let us suppose that four players are taking part in the game and that they hold the following cards:

	Mary A A K J	
John A J J K		Andrew A K Q J
	Q Q Q K Joan	

Each player selects a card he does not want and passes it face down to the player on his left. You must not wait to see the card you receive before passing on a card.

John would probably give his king to Mary, Mary might give her jack to Andrew, Andrew might give his own jack to Joan and Joan would certainly give her king to John. If anybody happens to start with four of a kind, he exposes his cards at once; but he does so quite quietly.

After each turn is complete the players look at their cards to see whether they now have four of a kind.

Mary, having received a king and parted with a jack, now holds two aces and two kings. She decides to pass an ace to Andrew and is glad she did so when John passes her another king. Mary now has three kings and is hopeful of collecting a fourth; but Andrew passes a queen to Joan, giving her four queens.

Joan quietly places her four queens face down on the table, and, in the excitement of the game, only John notices this. He places his own four cards on the table, while Mary passes a card to Andrew and Andrew passes a card to John. John passes the same card straight to Mary.

Where six or more are taking part, it is surprising how long some players take to notice that the game has been won.

The last player to place his cards on the table is the Donkey.

Players with four of a kind should be quick to place their cards on the table because there might be another player with four of a kind.

The winner is the player who is first to table four of a kind, but all players should be on the alert and ready to place their own cards on the table as soon as they see anyone else doing so.

Menagerie

This is a merry party game in the style of Snap, and the more there are the merrier it is likely to be.

The ordinary pack of fifty-two cards is used and the object of the game is to win all the cards.

Let us suppose there are only four players. Each player must represent an animal, so the names of four animals are written on four small pieces of paper—one on each—and each player draws to see which animal he represents. It is not necessary to write the names out in full, thus the letter E stands for elephant, K for kangaroo, and so on.

Here are the four players sitting round a table:

Alice
(Elephant)

Gordon
(Crocodile)

Tom
(Kangaroo)

Mary
(Hippopotamus)

Having drawn the highest card Tom deals the cards one at a time, face down, starting with the player on his left. With four players, each will be dealt thirteen cards, but if there were five players, two of them would have eleven cards and the others would have ten each. It does not matter if some players hold one card more than other players.

The players place their cards face down on the table in front of them in neat little stacks. The player on the dealer's left goes first; he turns over his first card—the top card of his stack—and places it face up on the table beside his stack. Then the next player turns over his top card and so on. Let us suppose that the first four cards turned over are

Mary	Gordon	Alice	Tom
♣ 5	♡ 7	♡ K	♠ 3

There are no matching cards as yet, so Mary places the next card from her stack face up on top of her five. (*See* plate 2). It happens to be a king, matching Alice's king. It now becomes a race between Mary and Alice to see which is the first to call out the other's animal name three times. Mary must call out 'elephant, elephant, elephant', and Alice must call out 'hippopotamus, hippopotamus, hippopotamus' as quickly as they can. It is easier to say 'elephant' than to say 'hippopotamus' which means that Mary has a good chance of being first; but Alice may have spotted the matching cards before Mary, or Mary may start to call out the wrong animal name. This time the winner happens to be Alice and she takes all the cards Mary has turned over (only two) and places them at the bottom of her stack.

It is now Gordon's turn. Perhaps five or six rounds of cards are turned over before two matching cards show up again, and now the race is well worth winning.

When a player comes to the end of his stack, he takes up his pile of turned-over cards and *they* become his stack.

Only the top card of each pile should be visible.

When a player has lost all his cards, he is out of the game. Eventually one player takes all the cards and, of course, wins the game.

Animal Noises

This is a variation of Menagerie. It is played in exactly the same way except that the players take the names of domestic animals: dog, horse, cat, sheep, duck, cow, and so on, and instead of calling out the animal name of the player with a matching card, the animal's own call noise must be imitated.

The players—this game is for the very young—should merely imitate the noise of the animal they represent. If Jim (cow) and Ted (duck) have matching cards, Jim must try to call out 'moo, moo, moo' before Ted can call out 'quack, quack, quack'.

Once the players have got well into the run of things, they can take on the slightly more difficult variation of imitating the animal noises of their opponents; thus Molly (dog) and George (cat) have matching cards. Molly must call out 'meow, meow, meow' before George can call out 'bow-wow, bow-wow, bow-wow'.

Old Maid

Any number from two to ten may play.

An ordinary pack of cards is used from which one of the queens is omitted.

The player who draws the highest card deals the cards, face down, one at a time to each player as far as they will go. It does not matter if some players hold a card more than other players.

Each player places on the table in front of him, and face down, all cards which pair. Thus if a player is dealt, say,

♠ 7 5; ♡ K 8 5; ◇ K 8 5 3; ♣ Q

he discards two fives, the kings and the eights, which leaves him with

♠ 7; ♡ none; ◇ 5 3; ♣ Q

When every player has completed the preliminary business of discarding all his paired cards, the player on the left of the dealer mixes his remaining cards and presents them face down to the player on his left. That player picks one card and if it pairs with any of his own cards, he discards the pair; otherwise he adds it to his hand, mixes and then presents his cards to the next player, and so on. This continues until every card but the odd queen has been paired off. The player left with the odd queen is the Old Maid.

The fact that a player is dealt an odd queen is of no immediate disadvantage, for he may draw another queen from the player on his right; or his odd queen may be picked from his hand by the player on his left.

Snap

From two to five may play.

An ordinary pack of 52 cards is used.

The player who draws the highest card from a spread pack deals first. He deals the cards as far as they will go, and it does not matter if some players hold a card more than other players. As usual the first card is dealt to the player on the dealer's left.

The object of the game is to win all the cards.

The players gather their cards into stacks, each player placing his stack face down in front of him. Each player in turn, beginning at the dealer's left, turns over his top card and places it face up on the table as the start of his Pile. Only the top card of each Pile should be visible.

When a player turns up a card that is of the same rank as a visible card on any other Pile, the first person to say 'Snap' wins both Piles and places them face down under his stack.

When a player has no more cards in his stack, he remains in the game and must be very much on the alert to call 'Snap' as soon as another player turns a card which matches his own top card. When a player loses his Pile and has no cards in his stack, he is out of the game.

A player who calls 'Snap' when cards of the same rank are not exposed has to give one card from his Pile to each of the other players.

Note. If, in turning over a card, a player turns it towards himself, he has the advantage of seeing it before the other players and has, therefore, a better chance of being the first to call 'Snap'. If, however, he turns the cards away from himself, he places himself at a disadvantage. It is best to turn over every card sideways.

Snip-Snap-Snorem

Any number may play.

An ordinary pack of 52 cards is used.

The dealer is the player who draws the highest card. He deals all the cards, face down, one at a time. It does not matter if some players have a card more than other players.

The object of the game is to get rid of cards as quickly as possible.

The player on the left of the dealer starts by placing any card face upwards on the table, say the queen of spades. If the next player on the left has a queen, he *must* play it and, as he does so, he cries 'Snip'. If he hasn't a queen, he says 'Pass' and it is the turn of the next player to play a queen or pass. (Play always goes to the left.)

The second, third and fourth queens are played sooner or later, the player playing the second queen saying 'Snip', the player playing the third queen saying 'Snap' and the player playing the fourth queen saying 'Snorem'. The 'Snorem' player leads to the next round.

If the leader or any other player holds more than one matching card, he must play them one after the other, not forgetting to say the appropriate words. Thus John leads a ten; Mary plays a ten and calls 'Snip'. If she has another ten she must play it and call 'Snap'. She may not hold it back to make a 'Snorem' card.

The first player to run out of cards wins the game.

Eights

From two to eight may play. Best for two, but quite good for three or four. When there are four players, each may play for himself or in partnership with one of the other three against the remaining pair.

An ordinary pack of 52 cards is used except when there are six or more players, when two packs, shuffled together, are used.

The player who draws the highest card from a spread pack deals, beginning with the player on his left. When there are two players only, each receives seven cards, face down, one at a time. When there are more than two players, each receives five cards. The remainder of the pack (or packs if more than five are playing)—the Stock—is placed face down in the middle of the table and the top card is placed face up beside the Stock and is called the Starter. If the Starter happens to be an eight, it is pushed into the Stock somewhere near the middle and the next card from the top of the Stock becomes the Starter unless it, too, happens to be an eight when it is buried about two-thirds down the Stock.

Beginning with the player on the left of the dealer, each player in turn plays one card face up on the Starter Pile. Each card thus played (the eights are exceptions—see below) must match the card currently showing on the Starter Pile either in suit or in rank. If, for example, the top card is the seven of hearts, the player whose turn it is to play must play either a seven or a heart. If unable or unwilling to play, he must draw a card from the Stock and continue to draw cards one at a time until he is able and willing to play, or until the Stock is exhausted. While there are cards in the Stock, a player in his turn may draw them even though he is able to match the card on the Starter Pile. Once the Stock is exhausted, however, players *must* play in turn if able; if unable to play, the turn passes to the next player.

Eights. The eights are 'wild', which simply means they are privileged cards and may be played no matter what the top card of the Starter Pile happens to be. When playing an eight, the player must declare the suit it represents. For example, the top card of the Starter Pile is the six of clubs. It is Tom's turn and he decides to play the eight of diamonds, which he may even though he has a club or a six, or even both. In playing the eight of diamonds, he declares that it is a spade, a heart, a diamond or a club, and the next player must either play a card of the declared suit or an eight.

The player who gets rid of all his cards first is the winner and collects from the other players the value of the cards they still hold. Suppose Tom goes out and the other two players are left with

	Mary		Dick
12	♠ A 7 4	67	♠ 9 8 5 3
50	♡ 8	5	♡ 3 2
18	◇ 10 5 3	10	◇ K
	♣ —	12	♣ 6 4 2

Mary has lost 80 counters. Dick has lost 94.
The scale is

Each eight	50
Each K, Q, J or 10	10
Each ace	1
Each other card	pip value

If none of the players is able to play after the Stock is exhausted, the player with the lowest total (according to the above scale) collects from each of the other players the difference of the totals.

In a partnership game, partners face each other. A game is not won until both members of the partnership get rid of all their cards. When one player goes out, the other three play on. If the game ends because none of the players is able to play, the side with the lower total wins.

Notes. If you have an eight in your hand when the game ends, it will cost you 50 counters; but eights can be very useful and you should often draw from the Stock rather than play an eight, especially in the early stages of play. Also it is a mistake to think that it is a disadvantage to hold more cards than the other players; it can be quite an advantage.

Suppose, for example, you and your opponent have these cards with the Stock exhausted:

You	Opponent
♠ 8	♠ 9 5
♡ K 10 7 6 3	♡ —
◇ Q 9 5	◇ —
♣ J	♣ 10 9

Your opponent leads the ten of clubs and you play the jack. Your opponent leads the nine of clubs and you play the carefully preserved eight of spades, declaring it to be a heart. Your opponent cannot play another card, for he has neither hearts nor diamonds. He is left with two spades and must pay you 14 counters.

If from the earlier play you thought your opponent had no red cards, you could have won 23 counters by playing your eight of spades on his ten of clubs, not forgetting to declare that it represents the heart suit. Now you play your hearts and diamonds and then go out by playing the jack of clubs.

Now give yourself three cards and leave your opponent with the same four:

♠ 10 7	♠ 9 5
♣ J	♣ 10 9

He plays a club, you play the jack. He plays his other club and you cannot go, so he plays a spade and you play a spade. He plays his last card and wins.

Go Fishing

Three to eight may play. The game is best when seven or eight play.

The player who draws the highest card deals out all the cards, face down, one at a time. It does not matter if some players hold one card more than other players. An ordinary pack of 52 cards is used.

The object of the game is to collect sets of cards—four of a kind. Four sevens, four kings, four fours and so on.

Any player who happens to have been dealt a set, places it face downwards on the table in a little pack.

The player on the left of the dealer has the first go. He may ask any one of the other players for a card, but he must hold at least one card of the same rank.

John, let us say, holds these cards:

♠ K 10 3
♡ K 7 2
◇ Q 8 5
♣ K 6

and asks Joan for the queen of clubs. He is, up to a point, lucky, for Joan happens to have this card and has to give it to John. John continues to fish for cards as long as he is successful, but as soon as his request for a card is denied, the turn passes to the next player on the left.

John may ask Joan or any other player for some other card; he badly wants the king of diamonds to make up a set, but is too wise to ask for it yet. He decides to ask Bill for the two of clubs. Bill hasn't this card, his hand being

♠ Q 7 6
♡ Q 8 6
◇ J 10 3 2
♣ 9

It is now the turn of the player on John's left to go fishing, and that player is Bill. Bill knows that John has the queen of clubs, for Joan gave it to him. He asks for, and receives, the queen of clubs. John must hold a card of the same rank, for he asked for the queen of clubs. So Bill asks John for the queen of diamonds and then places the four queens face down on the table. Bill makes a mental note of the fact that John has the two of spades and/or the two of hearts. Why? Because John asked for the two of clubs and Bill has the two of diamonds. Bill asks Hilda for the three of clubs, at which moment let us look at the cards held by John, Bill and Hilda:

John	Bill	Hilda
♠ K 10 3	♠ 7 6	♠ A J 5
♡ K 7 2	♡ 8 6	♡ A 10 4
◇ 8 5	◇ J 10 3 2	◇ None
♣ K 6	♣ 9	♣ J 10 7 2

There are two other players, Don and Lucy.

Hilda hasn't the three of clubs, so next on the left—Lucy—goes fishing and asks Hilda for the king of spades, unsuccessfully.

And so it goes on. Each player's request provides a clue to what he or she holds, and the game ends when all the sets have been collected and are on the table.

The player with most sets has caught the most fish and is the winner. If two or more players tie for first place with the same number of sets, the player with the highest ranking set is the winner. Aces are highest, then kings and so on.

I Doubt It

A game which adults and children can play together and thoroughly enjoy.

Any number from three to thirteen may play.

An ordinary pack of 52 cards is used for three, four or five players. With more than five players use two packs of cards shuffled together—it doesn't matter if the colours, or designs, on the backs are different.

The player who draws the highest card deals one card at a time, face down, as far as they will go. It does not matter if some players hold a card more than others.

The object of the game is to get rid of all one's cards.

Let us suppose there are five players: two of them will have 11 cards and the other three will have 10 cards.

The player on the left of the dealer has first go. He places from one to four cards face down on the table in front of himself and announces that they are aces. Any of the other players may challenge him, saying 'I doubt it'. If more than one player challenges, the one who challenged first is the official challenger. If two or more challenge simultaneously, the one nearest to the player's left is the official challenger.

After a challenge the player's cards which he declared were aces are turned face up. If they are aces, the challenger has to take them into his hand and he must also take into his hand any other cards which have been played and are on the table. If the cards are not *all* aces, the player must take them back into his hand together with any other cards which have been played on the table. If nobody challenges, the cards remain on the table until, at some later stage, a player (or a challenger) is compelled to take them into his hand.

After the first player's turn is completed, the next player to his left must put down one or two or three or four cards and announce that they are kings.

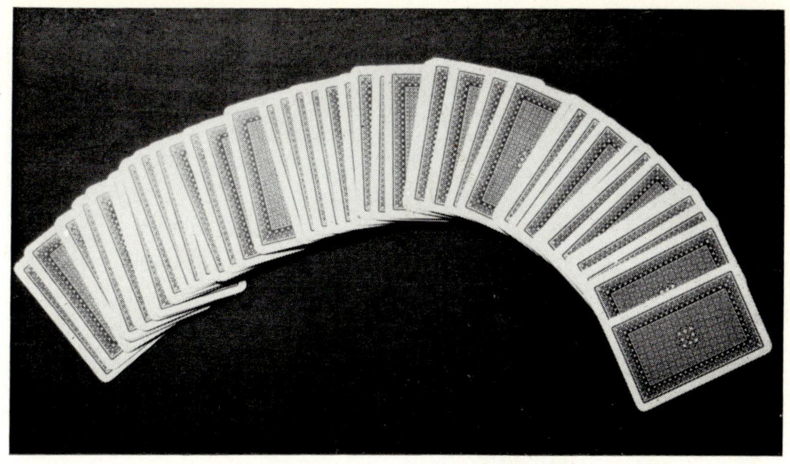

1. Preliminaries (see page 11)

2. Menagerie (see page 19)

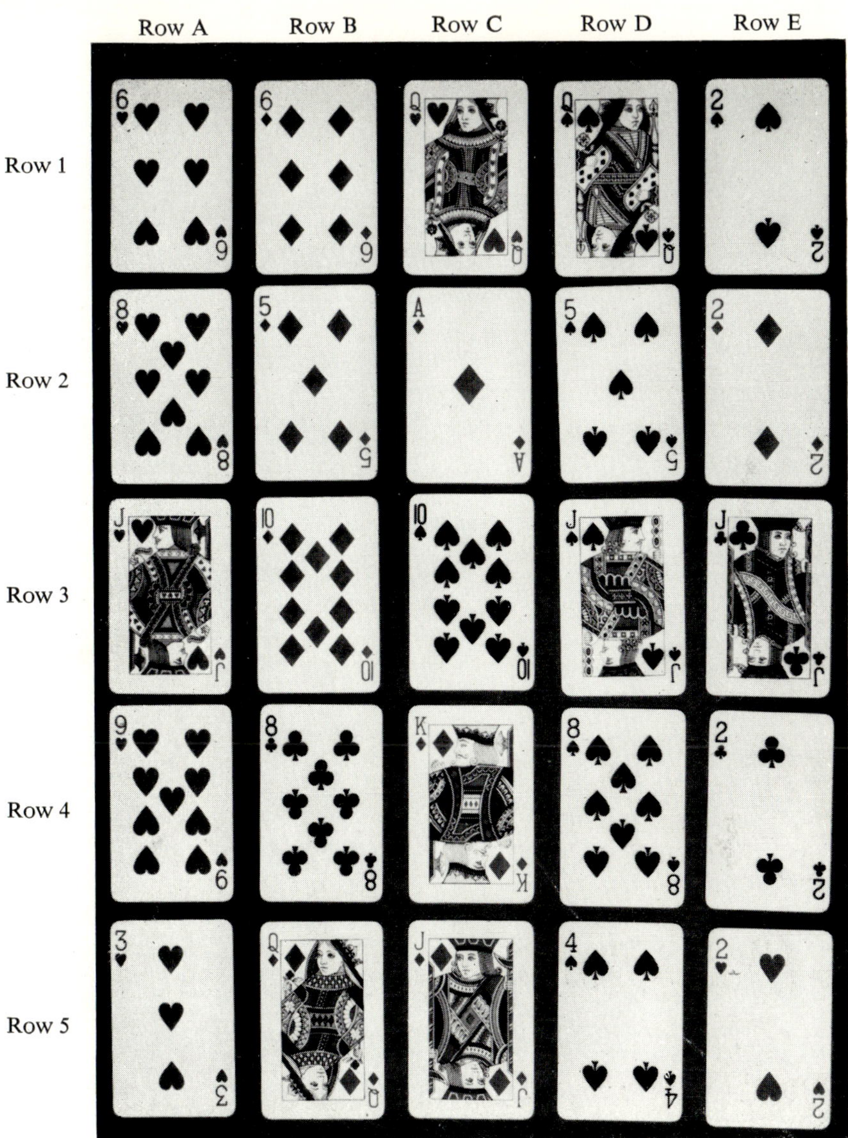

7. Poker Patience

I DOUBT IT

Let us play part of a game with five players. Mr Jones deals.

Mr Jones	Edward	Grace	Elspeth	Mrs Brown
A A	A	A	K	K
Q	K K	J J	Q Q Q	J J
10	10	10 10	9	8
8	9 9 9	8 8	7 7	7
6	7	5	6	4
5 5 5	6 6	4 4	4	3 3 3
3	2	2	2	2

As *we* look at the players Edward appears to be on the right of Mr Jones. In fact he is on the left, for the players are looking towards us. It is Edward to go first. He may place his lone ace on the table and declare one ace, but playing as safe as that will seldom allow him to get rid of all his cards first. Edward places his two kings face down on the table and says 'two aces'. If he had taken a bigger chance and put down his seven with the kings, hoping that the three unseen aces were divided one, one, one, he would have been challenged by Mr Jones who, holding two aces, would know that Edward could not hold three. As it is, nobody challenges; the cards are left face down on the table and it is now Grace's turn. Grace must announce kings even though she hasn't any. She places her tens on the table and announces two kings. Again nobody 'doubts it', so it is Elspeth's turn.

Elspeth places her queens on the table and announces 'three queens'. This is too much for Mr Jones who says 'I doubt it', whereupon Elspeth turns her three cards over and Mr Jones has to take them into his hand together with the two cards Edward played and the two cards Grace played.

Now it is Mrs Brown's turn. She places her jacks on the table and announces 'two jacks'. Grace, with two jacks, promptly says 'I doubt it', but Mrs Brown was not bluffing and Grace has to take those jacks into her hand, giving her four in all.

So it goes on until one player puts down his last card or cards and is either not challenged or, if challenged, has the cards he announced. He is the winner and takes the kitty into which every player has contributed twenty counters.

I DOUBT IT

The first turn is a call for aces, the next for kings and so on down to twos. If the game is still in progress after twos have been called, the next call is for aces again.

It is worth noting that Grace, who had to call kings, put her tens on the table. She could have put her eights if she had wished, but she had worked out that, on the next round, her call would be for eights. This is how the calls will fall to the five players in this game:

Mr Jones	Edward	Grace	Elspeth	Mrs Brown
	Aces	Kings	Queens	Jacks
Tens	Nines	Eights	Sevens	Sixes
Fives	Fours	Threes	Twos	Aces
Kings	etc.			

In his turn a player may put down from one to four cards, but they need not be all of the same rank. If the call is for eights, he may play a two, a three and a four and announce 'three eights'.

When two packs of cards are used (for more than five players), from one to eight cards may be played at each turn. The reason is, of course, that there are now eight cards of a kind.

I Fancy My Cards

Any number from two to twelve may play. Best for seven players.

An ordinary pack of 52 cards is used.

The dealer is the player who draws the highest card from a spread pack. He is also the banker and remains the banker for three rounds of deals unless the bank breaks.

Before play begins, the banker places a number of counters, say 25, in the kitty and deals three cards, face down, to the player on his left. All the remaining cards—called the Stock—are placed face down on the table in front of the dealer. Each player starts with 25 counters.

The player examines his three cards and if he thinks one of them will be in the same suit as, and higher than, the top card of the Stock, he says 'I fancy my cards to the tune of — counters', naming a number of counters not greater than (a) the number in the kitty, and (b) the number held by the player. If he thinks none of his cards has a chance of beating the top card of the Stock, he makes the minimum stake of one counter.

For example: Betty deals and gives the player on her immediate left (Mary) ♡ A K J. This is a poor hand. The Stock contains 49 cards, 10 are hearts and 39 are not hearts. So Mary has 10 chances of winning and 39 chances of losing. Quite rightly she says 'I fancy my cards to the tune of one counter.' Betty then turns up the top card of the Stock (say the two of spades), Mary turns over her three cards and her counter is added to the kitty. The four played cards are put to one side face down and form the beginning of the Discard Pile.

Betty deals to Tom: ♠ A Q; ♡ 5. If the top card of the Stock is a spade or one of the three lowest hearts, Tom will win. His chances are very slight, but he fancies his cards to the tune of three counters. Betty turns up the nine of clubs, Tom turns his three cards and the banker sweeps the played cards into the Discard Pile and the three counters into the kitty.

Betty deals to Jim: ♠ J; ♡ J; ♣ J. There are 29 counters in the kitty, but Jim only possesses 25 so he may not fancy for more than 25. He has a good hand, but will lose if Betty turns up a diamond or one of the three top cards in one of the other suits. But Jim remembers that ♡ A K Q and ♠ A Q are in the Discard Pile so he pushes forward 20 counters and says 'I fancy my cards for 20.' Betty turns up the 10 of spades and pays 20 counters out of the kitty to Jim who now has 45 counters. If, on the next time round, the bank had built up to 45 or more counters, Jim could fancy his cards for 45.

Betty deals to Lucy: ◇ A 9; ♣ 10. It is by no means even an average hand, but Lucky Lucy fancies her cards to the tune of nine. Betty turns up the four of hearts, and the kitty is increased to 18 counters.

As there are only five in the game, Betty starts her second round, giving three cards to Mary, and so on.

If the kitty runs out of counters, the bank passes to the next player on the left. The bank also passes if the banker completes three rounds of deals.

Whenever the Stock is exhausted, the banker gathers together the Discard Pile, shuffles the cards and places them to his right to be cut.

Before the new banker takes over there must be a reckoning. For example:

Betty, the banker, ends her third round of deals with a kitty of 53. She shows a profit of 28. Mary has a loss of 25 (having lost her last counter on the second round, Mary had to sit out for the third round). Tom has a loss of 12, Jim a gain of 23 and Lucy a loss of 14. These gains and losses are recorded on a sheet of paper and each player starts again with 25 counters.

The bank can be broken on the very first hand if the first player fancies her cards to the tune of 25 and wins, but a loss of all a player's counters puts him out of the game until the three rounds of deals have been completed.

This game is derived from the game of Slippery Sam.

The winner is the player with the largest credit balance after each player has had his turn as banker.

Nap

Two to six may play. The best number is four (or five).

A full pack of cards is used, the ace being high.

A game consists of any number of hands, but it is best to limit it to somewhere between 12 and 15. If there are four players, three rounds of deals will give 12 hands; with only three players, four or five rounds of deals may be played. It is as well to decide on the number of hands before starting.

The player who draws the highest card deals the first hand: five cards, face down, one at a time to each player.

Let us assume there are four players and that they hold these cards:

Keith	Harry	Mary	Lucy
♠ A 2	♠ K Q 10	♠ —	♠ —
♡ 10 5 4	♡ Q	♡ 6 3	♡ A J
◇ —	◇ J	◇ 10	◇ Q 3 2
♣ —	♣ —	♣ K 8	♣ —

Keith, on the left of the dealer, has the first go. He has to decide how many tricks he will win if he names his own trump suit, bearing in mind that only 20 of the 52 cards have been dealt. If he thinks that he will make less than two tricks, he passes. If he thinks he will make two tricks or more, he bids Two or Three or Four or Nap (Nap is all five tricks). He may make only one bid, and I confess that I would bid 'Three' on his cards. I would expect more often than not to make two hearts—the suit I would name as trumps—and the ace of spades. Keith is a more cautious player and simply says 'Two'. If none of the other players makes a higher bid, Keith plays against the rest and must first lead a card in his trump suit. Owing to the lie of the cards, Keith would probably make only two tricks. However, Harry makes a higher bid. He says 'Three'. If neither Mary nor Lucy makes a higher bid,

Harry plays the hand and names spades as the trump suit, hoping to make three spade tricks. If, as is likely, the ace of spades is one of the 32 undealt cards, Harry would be almost sure to make three tricks. As the cards lie he would be defeated in all probability.

It is now Mary's turn and she passes. Lucy, however, decides to take a chance and rather recklessly says 'Nap'. The player who makes the highest bid leads first, and Lucy's lead of the queen of diamonds indicates that diamonds are trumps. Both ace and king of diamonds are in the undealt portion of the pack, so the queen wins. Lucy continues with the three of diamonds and then the two. Then she plays the ace of hearts, followed by the jack; she makes all the tricks and lives up to her name of 'Lucky Lucy'.

The dealer is always the last to bid. If everyone before him has passed, he must make a bid of at least One. Nobody but the dealer may bid less than Two.

Scoring. When the final bid is One or Two or Three or Four and the player makes the number of tricks (or more) that he has bid, he receives from each opponent as many counters as the bid. If the bid is defeated, the bidder pays this number of counters to each opponent. Where, however, Nap is bid and made, each opponent pays 10 counters to the bidder; but the bidder only pays out six counters to each opponent if he fails to take all the tricks.

Each player should start with the same number of counters or dried beans or matches or whatever are used as counters.

The Play. A player must follow suit if he can. If unable to follow suit, he may play any card. A trick is won by the highest card played in the suit led, or, if the trick contains any trumps, by the highest trump. The winner of a trick leads to the next trick. As soon as a bid is made or defeated, play for that hand stops. Neither the bidder nor the opponents can gain by making extra tricks.

The Winner. If one player wins all the counters from the other players before the game ends, he is the winner. Otherwise the player at the end of the game who has most counters is the winner.

Variants. A bid of Misere ranks higher than a bid of three, but lower than a bid of four. If the hand is played in Misere, there are no trumps. The bidder leads first and must not make any tricks. If successful, he receives four counters from each opponent. If unsuccessful, he pays four to each. A bid of Wellington may only be made when an earlier Player bids Nap (which is short for Napoleon). Wellington outbids Nap, but the bidder has to pay 10 counters to each opponent if he fails to win all the tricks.

Note. The dealer, who is last to bid, may profit by being cautious, but the other players are unlikely to win in the long run if they adopt very cautious tactics. Take a look at another hand:

Mary	Lucy	Keith	Harry
♠ 7 6	♠ —	♠ —	♠ A 10 8
♡ K 2	♡ A 8	♡ —	♡ Q 10
◇ A	◇ J 8	◇ K	◇ —
♣ —	♣ Q	♣ A J 4 2	♣ —

Mary passes, Lucy bids two, Keith three and Harry four. Harry wins only three tricks, giving Keith and the others four counters each. Keith has lost eight counters through excessive caution. A bid of four on Keith's cards when only four people are playing is reasonable. Of course if Keith had been last to bid, it would be wiser to say only three provided the highest previous bid was only two.

Pelmanism

Any number may play, a fairly large table being most suitable.

When all who are taking part are seated, the player who draws the highest card (ace high) is the dealer. He shuffles all the cards and lays them out in any order and at any angle face downwards so that no card touches another. (*See* Plate 3.)

The object of the game is to collect pairs—two queens, two (or four) eights and so on.

The player on the left of the dealer turns over any two cards. If they chance to be a pair, he takes them and turns over two other cards. Whenever the two cards a player turns over do not form a pair, he turns them back again, being careful to leave them as near as possible exactly in their original positions. It is then the turn of the next player on the left to play.

At first it is complete guesswork, but, after a round or so, a player with a good memory—and especially a good photographic memory—should remember the positions of many cards which have been turned but not paired.

Suppose, for example, there are eight players in the game and that each has turned over and then turned back two cards; there are now 16 of the 52 cards which have been exposed for a second or two. It is again the player on the dealer's left to play, Tom. If Tom is new to the game or has not been watching carefully, he may turn over one of the 16 cards which has already been exposed. This is, of course, a wasted play. Or he may turn over a new card, the 17th to be exposed. It is, let us say, the three of clubs and Tom remembers that the three of hearts was turned over a few minutes ago almost directly opposite to him on the far side of the table. He turns over the card he thinks is the three of hearts, but finds it is the seven of spades. Back go the two cards to their original positions and it is now Margaret's turn. Quickly she turns over

Tom's three of clubs and then her hand goes unerringly to the three of hearts. Having collected the pair and placed it face down in front of her she turns over Tom's seven of spades and matches it with a previously exposed seven. Her play continues until she fails to form a pair.

Each player receives one counter from each of the other players for every pair he collects.

The Earl of Coventry

This game follows much the same course as Snip—Snap—Snorem, (*See* page 22) but is for slightly older children.

Any number may play.

An ordinary pack of 52 cards is used.

The player who draws the highest card deals the cards one at a time as far as they will go. It doesn't matter if some players have one card more than others.

The player on the dealer's left goes first. He can play any card he likes, but must begin with the first line of a verse of doggerel. Thus Tom plays the seven of hearts and says:

	'A horse was walking down the street.'
Helen: ♠ 7	'He had a friend whose name was Pete.'
George: ♣ 7	'And Pete had feet like plates of meat.'
Donald: ♢ 7	'The Earl of Coventry's horse was neat.'

The final line must include The Earl of Coventry, but no rhyming word may be repeated in any one verse. For example Donald could not say 'The Earl of Coventry's horse likes meat.'

The player who plays the fourth card has the next go:

Donald: ♢ K	'How can you say such a thing'
Mary: ♣ K	'That I will marry a king.'
Stephen: ♡ K	'Will you ask young George to bring
Dorothy: ♠ K	'The Earl of Coventry's ring.'

All the other players act as critics, and are usually outspoken. The final word in each line must rhyme and the lines should scan.

The player who gets rid of all his cards first is the winner.

Bridge—Two-handed

This is a modified form of bridge for two players.

Draw from a spread pack for deal. The player with the higher card deals first. Before the deal, the dealer shuffles and his opponent cuts for trumps. After cutting for trumps, he cuts again. The deal then proceeds.

Thirteen cards are dealt, face down, one at a time to each player. The remaining 26 cards are placed face down between the players. These cards are called the Stock.

The object of the game is to win as many *of the last thirteen tricks* as possible.

The dealer's opponent leads to the first trick; thereafter the winner of a trick leads to the next trick. A trick is won by the player playing the higher card of the suit led. A trick containing one trump is won by the trump.

Players must follow suit if able to do so. If unable to follow suit, the other player may play any card he wishes.

After each trick the players draw a card from the Stock, the winner of the trick drawing first. Tricks won while the Stock remains have no scoring value, but this is the time to try to build up a winning hand for the second period when tricks are scored.

When the last card of the Stock is drawn the players get down to the real business of trying to win as many tricks as possible.

Let us take a look at a game and assume that John has cut and that spades are trumps. The original hands in the first period are

Mary	John
♠ A J 6 4	♠ 7 5 2
♡ K Q 10 3	♡ 8 5 4
◇ J 7	◇ Q 9 6 4
♣ A K J	♣ Q 7 6

With this very poor hand John seems to have little hope. He plans to take away some of Mary's probable strength by leading trumps whenever possible. He leads the two of spades, which Mary wins with the four. Mary draws the nine of hearts from the Stock and John draws the useful three of spades (trumps). Mary leads the seven of diamonds and John deliberately takes the trick simply in order to lead another trump. By plugging away with low trumps, John hopes he is undermining the stronger hand. With only two cards left in the Stock, the players hold

Mary	John
♠ K 8	♠ Q 10
♡ A K Q 10	♡ 9 8 2
◇ 10 5	◇ A K 8 6 3 2
♣ A K 7 6 5	♣ 8 2

It is John's lead and although the trick—the last in this period—will not score anything, John believes that it is of the utmost importance to win it, so he leads the ace of diamonds and Mary has to follow suit. John draws the nine of clubs from the Stock and Mary the six of hearts. From this stage each player strives to win as many tricks as he can.

John leads the king of diamonds and continues with the eight. Mary wins with the eight of trumps, plays the king of trumps and then leads hearts. Unable to follow suit when the fourth heart is led, John trumps with the queen of spades and makes his four remaining diamonds. He is left with ♣ 9 8 2, while Mary has ♣ A K and the six of hearts. Mary wins the last three tricks, a total of eight to her and five to John. The difference is three tricks and one point is awarded for each.

The winner is the player who first scores ten points.

If John had not bothered to take the last of the non-scoring tricks, he would have been heavily defeated. If, say, he leads the eight of clubs instead of the ace of diamonds, Mary should win and now she draws first from the Stock. Her card is the nine of clubs, while John draws the six of hearts, leaving this position:

Mary	John
♠ K 8	♠ Q 10
♡ A K Q 10	♡ 9 8 6 2
◇ 10 5	◇ A K 8 6 3 2
♣ A 9 7 6 5	♣ 2

Mary leads the king of spades, for she remembers that the ace has been played earlier. Then she leads the ace of clubs and continues with the nine (or she may play her four hearts first). John plays the queen of spades on the nine of clubs and is able to make two top diamonds. Mary trumps the next diamond and the rest of the tricks are hers, a total of ten to John's three: seven points to Mary.

John's very good play with rather poor cards saved him four points. Indeed John's play is a fine example to everyone who holds poor cards to fight on. Never, never, never give up.

Fall Out

From four to six may play.

Each player places 12 counters in the kitty.

An ordinary pack of 52 cards is used, the ace being high.

The player who draws the highest card from a spread pack deals; he cuts for trumps and the player on his right cuts for the deal.

The dealer distributes the cards in the ordinary way, face downwards, one at a time, starting with the player on his left.

If there are four players, each receives four cards; if five players, five cards; if six players, six cards each. The undealt cards, called the Stock, are placed in the middle of the table, face down.

The player on the dealer's left leads any card. The players must always follow suit if they can. If unable to follow suit, any card may be played.

A trick is won by the player playing the highest card of the suit led. If the trick contains any trumps, it is won by the player playing the highest trump.

The winner of a trick takes the top card of the Stock and leads to the next trick. Only the winner of a trick draws from the Stock.

When a player has no more cards, he falls out. The last player to have any cards is the winner and collects all the counters in the kitty. If there are two or more players, *all* of whom play their last card to the same trick, the winner of the game is the player who wins the last trick.

The players contribute a further 12 counters to the kitty for the next game. The deal passes to the left.

Here is a sample of how the play *might* go:

Rose	Jane	Tom	Mary
♠ 7	♠ 10	♠ 8	♠ 4
♡ A	♡ —	♡ Q 3	♡ 5
◇ A	◇ 8	◇ —	◇ 3 2
♣ A	♣ J 2	♣ 10	♣ —

FALL OUT

Spades are trumps. Lucky Rose and unlucky Mary you might say. Rose should win easily; it is her lead and she chooses the ace of hearts. Not having a heart, Jane plays her 10 of spades and wins the first trick. From the Stock she draws the eight of clubs. Jane leads the eight of diamonds, Tom trumps and wins the trick. From the Stock Tom draws the two of hearts, then he leads the queen of hearts. Not having a heart, Rose trumps and wins the trick. She draws the nine of clubs from the Stock and leads the ace of clubs. Mary has only one card, the four of trumps. She wins the trick and draws the four of hearts from the Stock. The four players each hold one card and it is Mary's lead. The cards are

♣9 ♣8 ♡2 ♡4

So Mary's four of hearts wins the last trick and Mary takes all the counters in the kitty.

Rose would have been wiser to lead the seven of spades. As the cards lie, she would have lost this trick, but would have won the next three at which stage Tom and Mary would have had to fall out. Jane, with only the eight of clubs, would lose the next trick to Rose's nine of clubs (or four of hearts if she preferred to lead a heart) and Rose would be the winner.

Newmarket

From three to eight may play.

A full pack of cards *plus four cards from another pack* are used.

The player who draws the highest card from a spread pack deals first.

The four cards from another pack are called the Boodle Cards. They are

♡A ♣K ◇Q ♠J

and are placed face up in the middle of the table where they remain throughout the game.

Before the deal each player places one counter on each Boodle Card except the dealer who places two counters on each.

The cards are cut and dealt one at a time to the left; one extra hand is dealt, immediately on the left of the dealer.

If there are five players, six hands are dealt. Four of the six hands will contain nine cards (36 cards) and the other two hands will contain eight cards each.

No player may see the cards in the extra hand.

The player on the dealer's left plays first. He may play a card from any suit, but it must be the lowest card in the suit he selects. The player holding the next higher card in the same suit plays it, then the next higher card is played and so on until the suit is stopped either because the ace of the suit is played or because the next higher card is reposing in the extra hand. In either case the player who played the last card must lead a new suit, and the lowest card he holds in that suit. If he only has cards in the suit which has just been stopped, the lead passes to the player on his left.

When a player is able to play a card which is the same as one of the Boodle Cards, he takes all the counters from that card.

The objects are to get rid of all your cards and to collect as many

Boodle Card counters as possible. The player who is first out receives one counter from the others.

If at the end of a game, the counters on one or more of the Boodle Cards have not been collected, they remain until won in a subsequent game. Sometimes matching Boodle Cards are in the extra hand and cannot be played. Sometimes a player holds one or more matching Boodle Cards and is unlucky enough not to get the chance of playing them.

In every new deal the dealer places two counters on the Boodle Cards, the other players placing one on each. Naturally the sooner a game ends when you haven't any Boodle Cards, the better for you.

Let us suppose that it is Henry's go and that he decides to lead a diamond. The five players hold 11 of the 13 diamonds:

Henry	Mary	Charles	Susan	Tom
◇ 9 8 6	◇ 5 4 2	◇ Q 7	◇ K 10	◇ A

Henry leads his lowest diamond, the six; Charles plays the seven; Henry the eight and nine; Susan the ten. Charles is on the verge of winning the counters on the ◇ Q Boodle Card, but is unlucky. The ◇ J is in the extra hand so the suit is stopped and Susan leads a new suit, and her lowest card in that suit. Of course Charles might play a stop card later on and would then be allowed to lead his lowest card in some other suit. Naturally he would promptly play the queen of diamonds.

Oh! Well

Three to seven may play. Each plays for himself.

The player who draws the highest card is the dealer of the first hand. He shuffles the cards and cuts them, exposing the card he has cut. The exposed card fixes the trump suit for this hand. The pack is then cut for the deal by the player on the dealer's right.

When there are four players, the 52 cards are dealt, 13 to each player.

When there are three players, the dealer removes the bottom card and puts it to one side unseen. Now 51 cards are dealt, 17 to each player.

When there are five players, the dealer removes the two bottom cards and places them (unseen) to one side. The remaining 50 cards are dealt, 10 to each player.

When there are six players, the dealer removes the four bottom cards and places them (unseen) to one side. Now there are only 48 cards, eight being dealt to each player.

When there are seven players, the three bottom cards are removed and placed to one side unseen. The remaining 49 cards are dealt, seven to each player.

The cards are dealt one at a time to each player starting with the player on the dealer's left.

The players examine their cards and then declare—starting with the player on the left of the dealer—*exactly* how many tricks they will try to take.

Suppose there are five players. Each will receive 10 cards and there will be 10 tricks. One player, selected by vote, writes down the names of the players and the number of tricks each declares to make:

John says five.

Joan says three.

Edward says six.

Susan says none.

Gwyneth says eight.

The player on the dealer's left leads any card he likes to the first trick and each player must follow suit if he can. If a player is unable to follow suit, he may play any card. The highest card in the suit led wins the trick. If there are any trumps in a trick, the highest trump wins the trick.

A player who wins a trick leads to the next trick. Each player must keep beside him the tricks he has won.

If a player wins the exact number of tricks he declared, he receives ten points. Where a player declared, and succeeded in making, no tricks, he receives 12 points.

Game. A game consists of two complete rounds of deals except when there are only three players, when three complete rounds of deals are played. Thus with three players 9 hands are played; with four players 8 hands; with five players 10 hands; with six players 12 hands; with seven players 14 hands. By agreement a game of seven players may be reduced to one complete round of deals: seven hands.

Where five players are taking part, the score after one round of deals might be something like this:

Hand	*1*	*2*	*3*	*4*	*5*
John	0	10	10	10	0
Joan	0	0	10	0	12
Edward	0	0	0	0	0
Susan	12	0	10	10	10
Gwyneth	10	0	0	0	10

Poor Edward has not scored yet, but there are five more hands to go and 'never say die' is the motto for those who play and enjoy games of cards. Who knows what may happen? On the first hand of the second round of deals Edward may declare 10 tricks and make them, scoring 20 points.

Notes. The deal passes to the left as in nearly every card game, and the new dealer must shuffle the cards, not forgetting the two which were removed. He cuts for trumps and the cards are then cut again for the deal by the player on the dealer's right. Two cards are again removed from the bottom of the pack if there are five players and the procedure is as before, the players making their new declarations.

The winner is the player who has most points at the end of the game. If two or more players have the same number of points, the player who was the first to score is the winner. If two or more players scored their first points at the same time, they are joint winners.

If in the above game John and Joan finished first with the same number of points, John—having scored first—would be the winner.

A player is entitled to be informed at any time how many tricks any other player has declared to win and how many tricks each player has won. Players should keep their tricks so that it is possible to see quite easily how many they have. (*See* Plate 4.)

Patience—Rescuing Cards

This patience is devised for one person, but can be played as a game in which others take part (see below).

From an ordinary pack of cards remove all twos, threes, fours, fives and sixes; this leaves 32 cards.

Shuffle and then deal the cards in four horizontal rows of eight, eight, eight and then seven in the bottom row. These 31 cards are dealt face down. The 32nd card starts the patience.

The object is to rescue as many cards as possible.

The top row of eight is reserved for the spade suit, the second row for the heart suit, the third and fourth rows for diamonds and clubs respectively.

The left-hand card of each row is reserved for the ace, the next card in the row is reserved for the king, then the queen and so on down to the seven.

Let us suppose that the 32nd card is the eight of hearts. The allotted position for the eight of hearts is the seventh card in the second row; so the face-down card occupying this position is taken up and the eight of hearts is placed face upwards in its rightful position. The taken-up card is, let us suppose, the jack of spades. The card occupying this position (fourth card in the top row) is removed and the jack of spades takes its place, face up. The removed card is, say, the ten of diamonds. It is placed in its correct position (fifth card in the third row) and we will assume that the face-down card we remove from this position is the dreaded seven of clubs. (*See* Plate 5.)

The game ends as soon as this card is turned up, so this has been a very short and unsuccessful patience, only three cards having been rescued.

If you can rescue 16 to 18 cards before the seven of clubs turns up, you have scored reasonably well. Rescuing 19 to 24 cards is very good.

Rescuing more than 24 is excellent. If the very last card to be turned up is the seven of clubs, you have rescued all the cards and gained a great victory. The odds against this splendid feat are 31 to one.

As a game, half a dozen or more may take part provided there is sufficient floor space and sufficient packs of cards.

Each player places 12 counters in the kitty and, after removing all the twos, threes, fours, fives and sixes, each player shuffles and cuts his own pack and the game begins. The winner is, of course, the player who rescues most cards, and he wins the kitty. In the event of a tie, the kitty is divided.

Poker Patience

From one to any number may play. Each player requires a complete pack of 52 cards.

The object of the game is to place 25 cards in five rows of five and to build 10 Poker hands, five in the vertical rows and five in the horizontal rows. I will first explain what happens when only one person is playing.

The best Poker hand, and the highest scoring one, is a Straight Flush. It consists of five cards of the same suit and in sequence, such as ♠ 6 7 8 9 10 or ♡ 2 3 4 5 6. The four top straight flushes, A K Q J 10 of the same suit, are called Royal Straight Flushes.

The next best hand consists of four matching cards, say four queens or four sevens. The term used is Four of a Kind.

Next in order is a Full House, which is three of a kind and one pair. This sort of thing: K K K 8 8 or 6 6 6 J J.

A Flush consists of five cards, all of the same suit.

A Straight is a sequence of five cards in different suits.

Three of a Kind comes next: three fours or three aces for example.

The penultimate hand in the list consists of two pairs and the last hand contains just one pair.

SCORE TABLE

Royal Straight Flush	50
Straight Flush	36
Four of a Kind	24
Full House	12
Flush	10
Straight	7
Three of a Kind	5
Two Pairs	3
One Pair	1

After shuffling and cutting, the player turns up the two top cards and places them face up on the table so that one is immediately above or below or to either side of the other, or corner to corner with it.

The next 23 cards are taken from the top of the pack one at a time, but not until the previous card has been placed. A card cannot be moved from the position in which it is placed once a new card is turned up.

Let us suppose that the first nine cards have been placed as illustrated in Plate 6.

Row 1: Two Pairs	3	Row A: Flush	10
Row 2: One Pair	1	Row B:	0
Row 3: Full House	12	Row C: Straight	7
Row 4: One Pair	1	Row D: Flush	10
Row 5:	0	Row E. Four of a Kind	24

This—68—is not a bad score, particularly as the cards did not come out too well for the player.

The best possible score in Poker Patience is 370; it is made up of five Royal Flushes and five Fours of a Kind.

If more than one is taking part, the players draw from a spread pack for 'deal'. The 'dealer' calls out the first two cards and subsequently turns the cards and announces them one at a time. The players (other than the 'dealer') should sort their cards into suits and in numerical order. This will help them to find the cards called out by the 'dealer' without unnecessary delay.

As soon as all the players have placed the first two cards, the 'dealer' turns up and announces the next card, and so it goes on until 25 cards have been turned and placed.

At the completion of a game, each player adds up and records the score for each of his rows and passes the score to another player to check. The player with the highest score is the winner. Each lay-out will consist of the same 25 cards, but it is improbable that any two will be alike.

Patience—The Shuffle

The Shuffle is a simple patience game.

An ordinary pack of 52 cards is used.

Turn the first four cards face up and place them in a horizontal row. From this row remove any card which is inferior to any other card in its own suit.

Deal four more cards on top of the original row whether on cards or in spaces. Remove, as before, any cards which are of inferior rank to any card of the same suit which is showing.

For example:

1st row ♣ A ♡ 7 ♣ K ◇ 8

Remove the king of clubs and deal another row on top of the first row:

2nd row ◇ 7 ♡ 4 ◇ 3 ♠ 6

Remove the three of diamonds, thus creating a space, for there was no first row card under the three of diamonds. In the space thus provided you may place any exposed card (the ◇ 7 or the ♡ 4 or the ♠ 6). If you move the ◇ 7, you will have this exposed row:

♣ A ♡ 4 ◇ 7 ♠ 6

which is not of the slightest use. But if you move the ♡ 4, you get this row:

◇ 7 ♡ 7 ♡ 4 ♠ 6

and away goes the four of hearts. Fill the blank space with the six of spades and it uncovers the eight of diamonds. Now you can remove the seven of diamonds which leaves you with

Void ♡ 7 ♠ 6 ◇ 8

The object is to leave the four aces in the row, all the cards of inferior rank being massed in a heap in front of the player, which is a very good way of shuffling the pack.